Things That Move in the Arctic

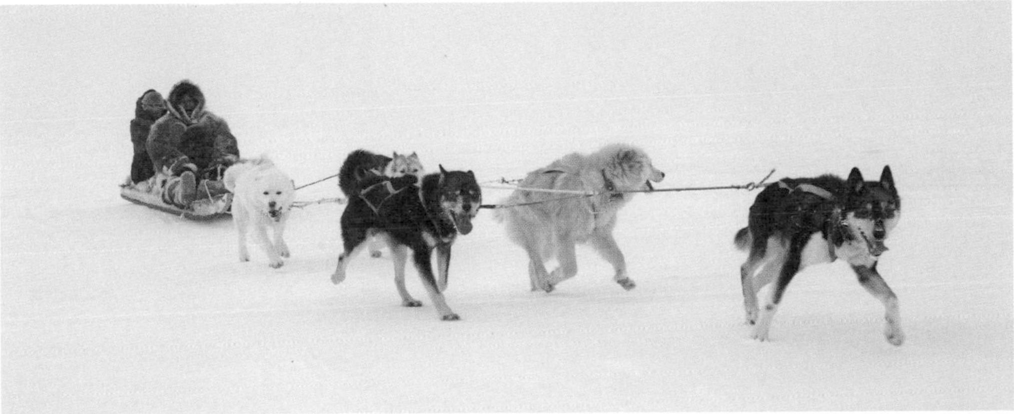

snowmobile

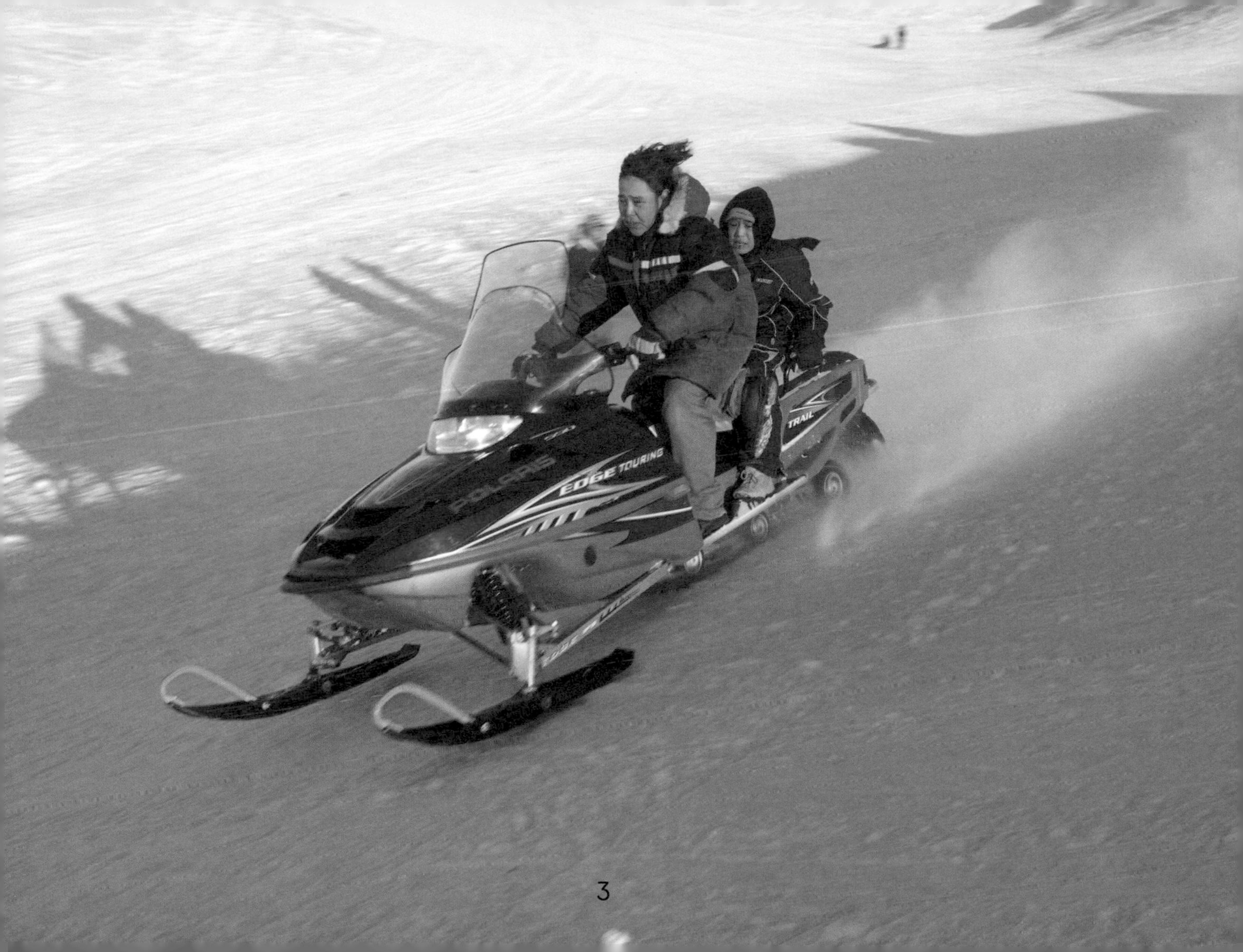
POLARIS
EDGE TOURING
TRAIL

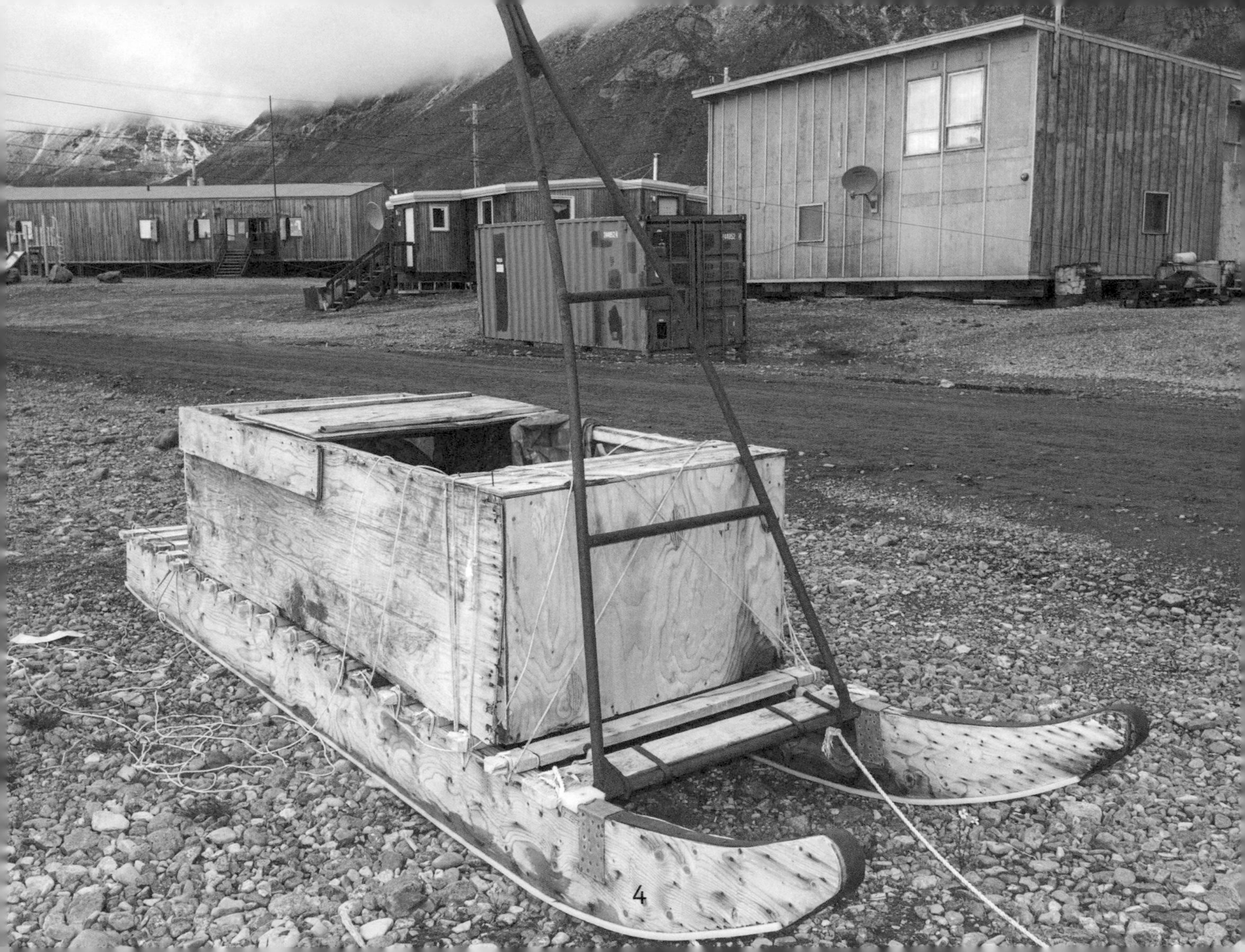

qamutiik

truck

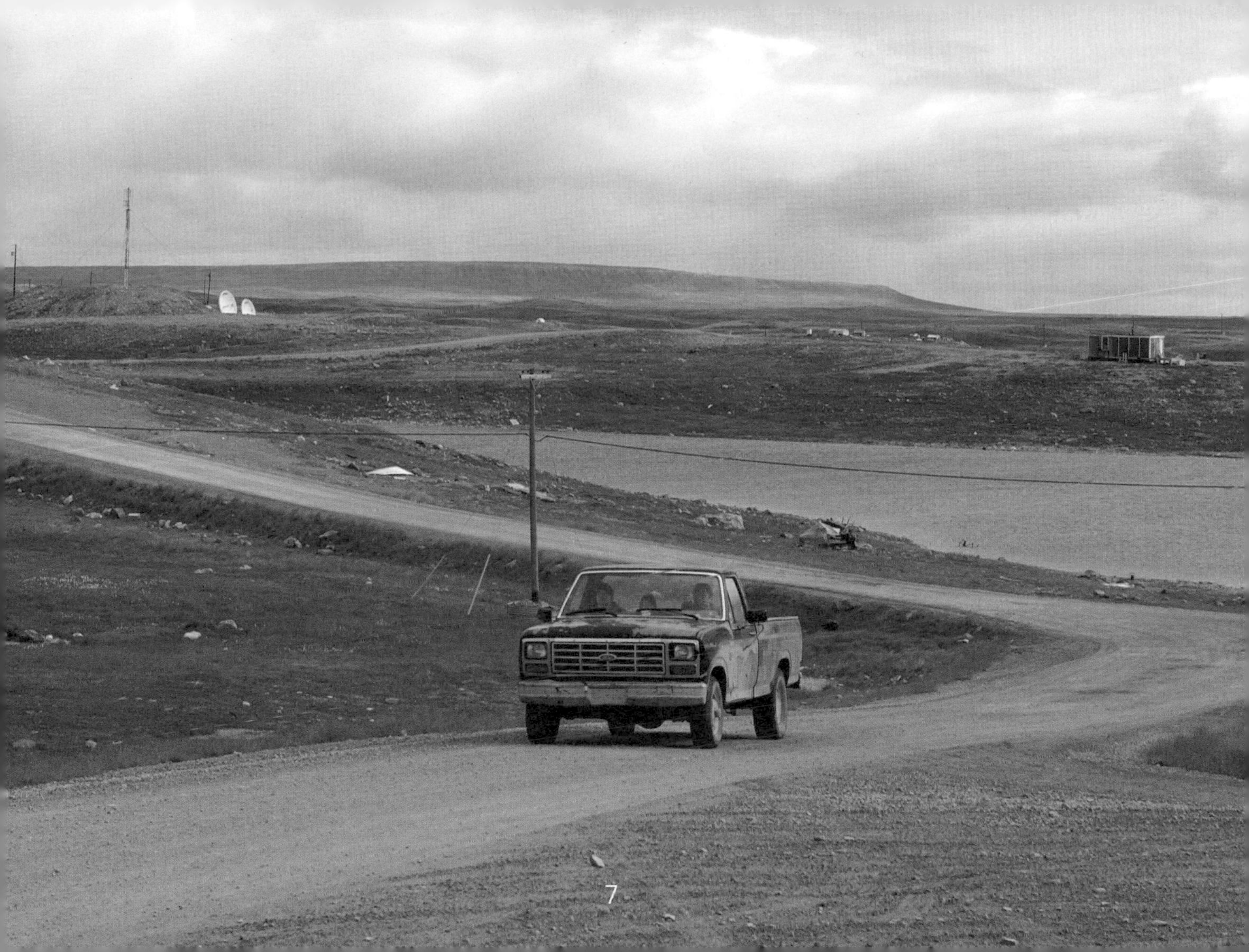

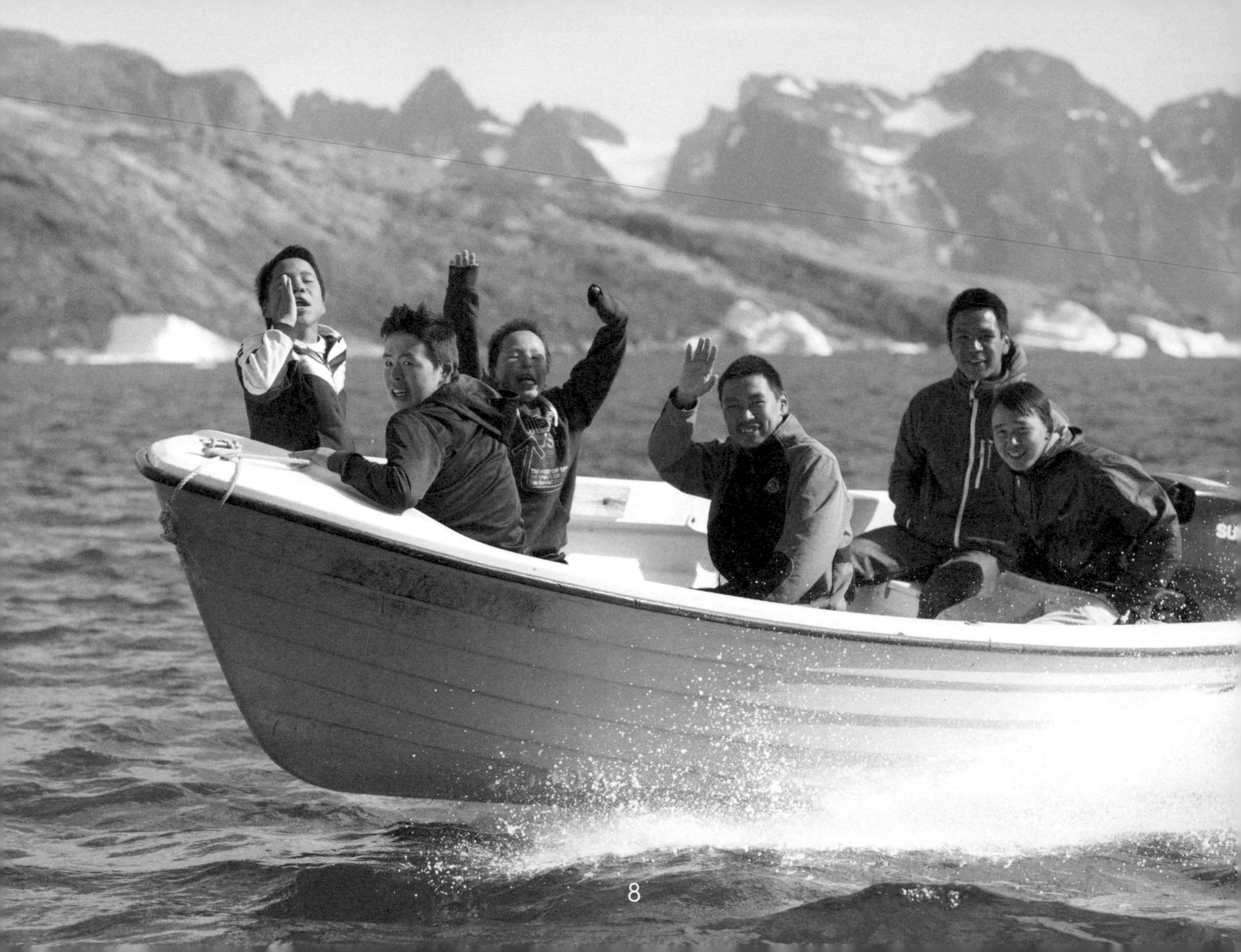

boat

qajaq

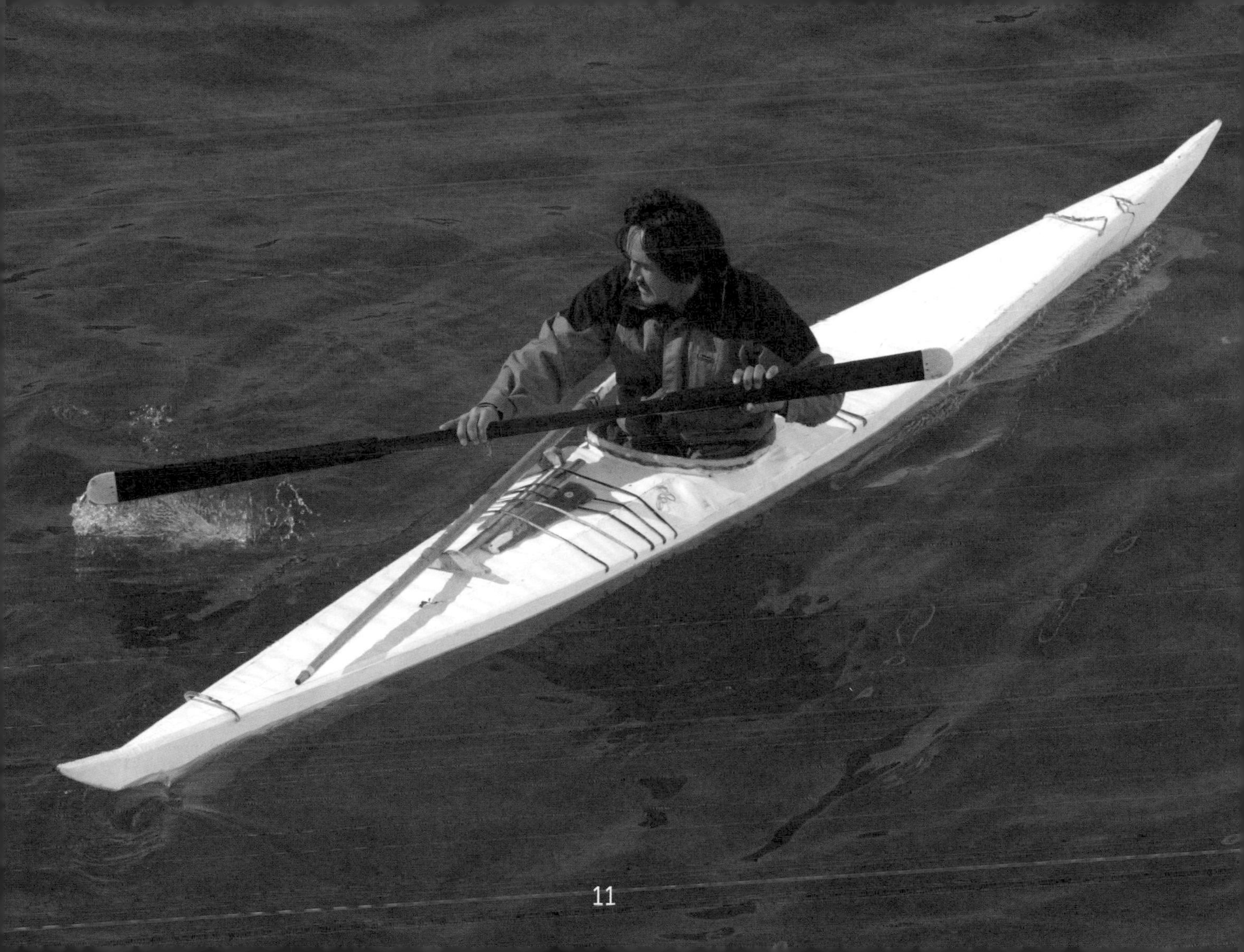

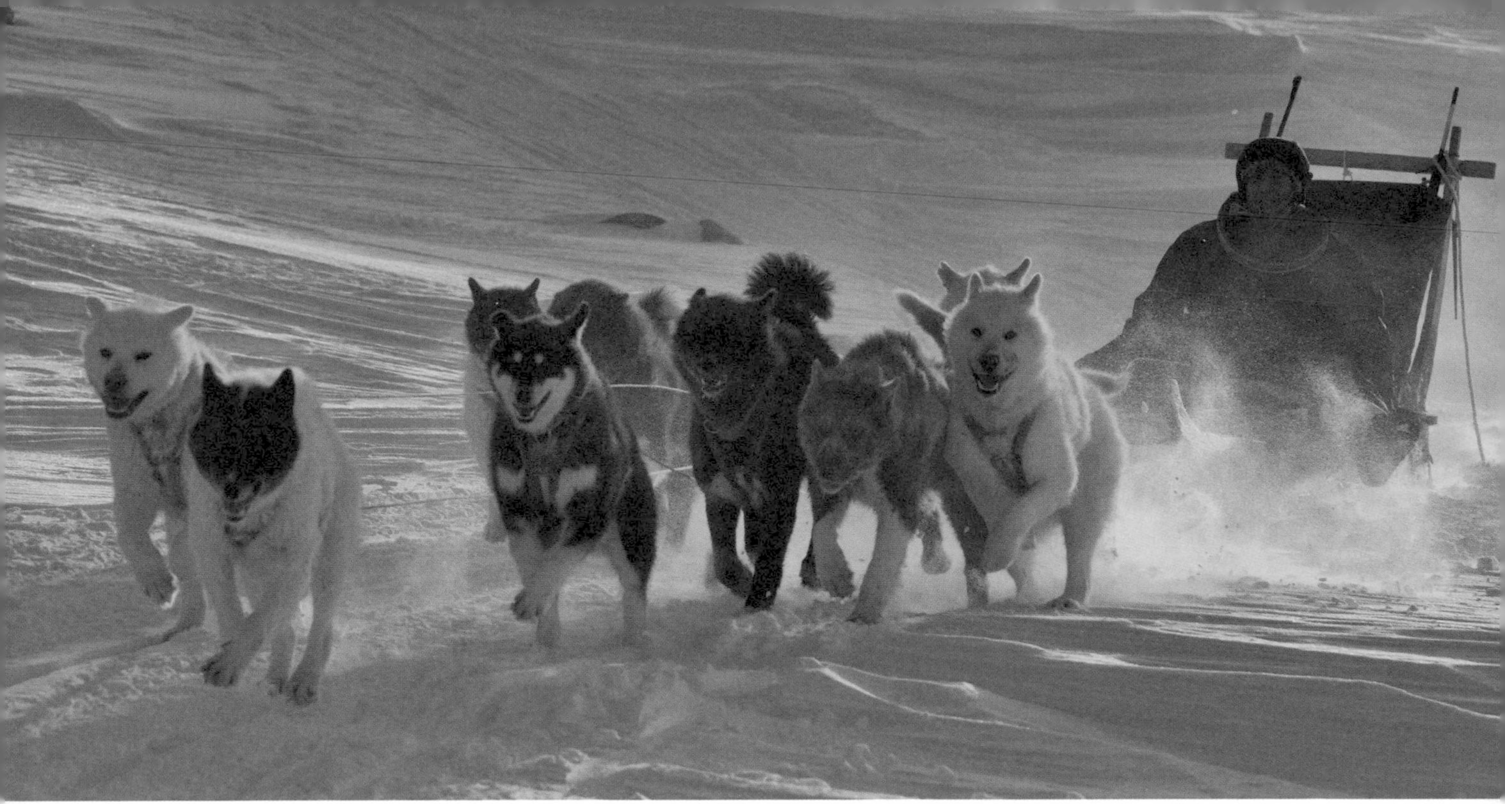

dog team